## Sn

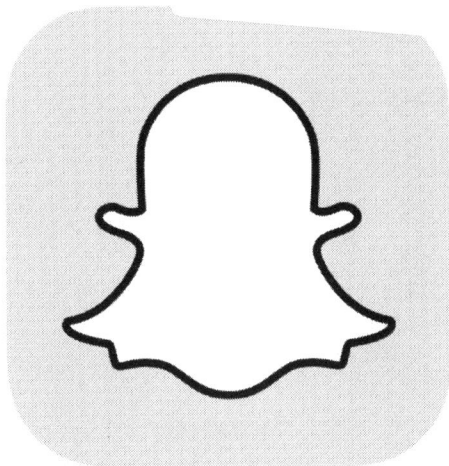

# Complete Guide to Using Your Snapchat to It's Fullest:

# Tips & Secrets Guidebook

# Contents

# Understanding Snapchat

Snapchat is a free to download app where users can send photo, videos and text messages. This app was launched in 2011 and is continuously gaining popularity since then. The unique feature of this app is that the content, whether photo or video sent through this app lasts only for few minutes and disappears after some time. In case, you want to save the message then you can take its screenshot and save in some folder for future reference. As per reports, in May 2014, around 700 million snaps were sent in a day and that number is increasing day by day. Due to this fame and instant popularity, Facebook offered $3 billion for acquiring Snapchat. However, this offer was soon turned down by its founder. Facebook, then launched a similar app called Slingshot, which in fact failed subsequently.

Photo credits: http://blogdebori. com/wp-content/uploads/2015/08/snapchat-portada-660x360. jpg

# Snapchat Potential users?

Social sites and other apps are evolving at a faster rate to match up with the ongoing trend of the social networking market. People of any age can start using Snapchat, but mainly this app is created for teenagers and adults. Snapchat users are increasing in every field and area, but this app was mainly intended for teenagers. Another app called Vine makes use of one of the features of this Snapchat app called Story feature in order to communicate with the fans and followers.

# Some Basic Terms

*For Beginners, we will discuss some the terms which are used in Snapchat app*

**Snapchatters:** People who actively use Snapchat app are called Snapchatters

**Snaps:** This is a well-known term and represents photos or videos, which are taken using this app.

**Snapback:** Refers to the reply of the recipient given to snap.

**Story:** A Snapchat message can be broadcasted to social media or your follower's. This message can be viewed multiple times in 24 hours, and a story can be created containing messages received in this 24 hours' time.

**Scores:** This represents your total score or amount of snaps sent and received . You can easily check your score next to your Display name from contact list of any of your friends.

**Chat:** Live or offline exchange of messages.

**Here:** This feature allows you to start live video chat while sending message directly.

# Know some HOW'S ?

Photo credits: http://www. revista. espiritolivre. org/wp-content/uploads/2014/01/snapchat. jpg

As we already cleared Snapchat, a video and picture sending app which is free, both of these picture and video destructs after few seconds when a person is viewing them.

This is rather a fun app for messaging. You can send amazing photos or videos to your friends and relatives by clicking beautiful pictures and adding a caption or doodle or lens graphics over the top of message screen. You may add these photos and videos to your story containing collection of your whole day or 24-hours photos and videos, which can later be broadcasted either publically or to your followers.

Snapchat as the name suggests is considered best for sending snaps or photos inculcating various features to beautify the image professional style. Almost 10 seconds, image will be displayed on screen and will self-destruct after this period. In case, you want to see images in future, you can take snapshot .

How you can save your photos sent through snapchat will be revealed in later pages of the book.

If you are really keen to know about What and How Snapchat works and How you can use it, keep going through the pages and see the magic of this new app.

## How you can start accessing Snapchat?

It is true that Snapchat is simple but it is at times confusing too.

Main screen of this app is the camera view screen of your mobile which sometimes makes difficult to access the app and navigate around. Maintain your patience level and stay calm and keep reading and following instructions in order to learn tactics of using Snapchat app. This app is simple and you can easily master it through few tutorials.

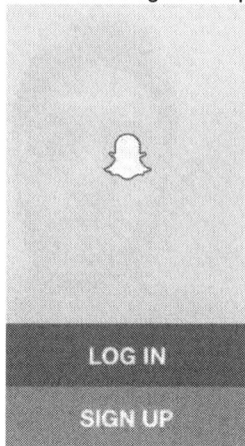

Photo credit: http://i.stack.imgur.com/esxrR.Jpg

# Main screen

This first step to access this app is to get it in your mobile. For this, you need to download it and remember, it is free to download. Create your ID like you do while creating any new account on other sites. Once you get your user ID, you can access this app. This app will take you to camera view screen as that is the main screen.

You will find flash located at the extreme left-hand corner of the screen that comes with toggling option in case you want to switch it off. Extreme right side of main screen has toggling button for switching from front or rear camera and vice versa. You will find camera view at the center.

Picture or videos can be clicked using the round camera button provided at the bottom of the camera view. You simply need to hold this button down in case, you want to record a video along with the sound, or simple tapping on this button allows you to take pictures.

Square icon provided on the extreme left side of bottom part displays the number of unread snaps, which are waiting for you. You can either Tap or Swipe it from left to mark them read or send a message to friends and relatives.

3-line icon or sometimes "+" is for stories provided at the extreme right art bottom side, which can be tapped or swiped from right in order to view stories or watch contents from various publishers such as ESPN, Food Network and many more.

## How to access Contacts List?

If you want to open contact screen, tap on Snapchat logo and if you want to add contacts, swipe screen down while staying on main screen. You can easily access settings option through the icon provided at the top right side. You can see list of people who have added you as friend, you can find new friends to add and do browsing of all friends.

Your account name will appear just below the snapchat logo. Score Count can be checked just next to your account name. Snapchat logo can be changed and customized via tap to add your favorite picture or selfies.

If you don't want to do anything with the contacts, simply swipe screen from the bottom to make a smart exit.

Photo credit: http://acmos.net/wp-content/uploads/2013/07/317086_397218963706400_737118848_n-300x300.Png

## How to make Snaps?

If you want to start taking snaps, simply tap the large button of the camera to click snap. For video, you can hold the button for some time. Preview option allows customize snaps, adjust its length or send to any friend and so on.

This preview screen comes with an X icon provided on top left corner of the screen. In case, you are done and want to return to the main screen, tap that X icon to get back to the main screen. There is one more pencil like button for customization, tapping it on top right-hand side will give you a color slider.

You can select any color using your fingers and start drawing things you want to see on the snap which was displayed in earlier screens. You can even access keyboard by tapping anywhere in the screen with preview to add some text. This feature is pretty simple yet interesting.

You can also add filters in preview screen depending upon your location, timings, temperature and speed with which you are moving. You can even change the color and style of your snap by swiping across the screen.

When you are done with all the above steps, you will see settings for adjusting length of your snap. This icon is provided at the left side of the screen in circular shape containing numbers representing number of seconds, recipients can see your snap. This icon can be tapped to make adjustment of snap length from 1 to 10 seconds.

This icon for snap length is a universal one and can be downloaded easily without facing any issues. Selecting it will give your snap on your system. Other icon provided at the bottom of camera view screen is for stories that will be discussed later on.

## How to Send Snaps?

There is one more icon that left unattended in preview section of this app and that is arrow-shaped icon called Send Snap icon provided at the bottom right-corner of the screen. Simply Tap it and send your snap to any of your friend. This will open a send-to option screen that allows you to select recipient's name. After you have done this, you can easily send your snap to your friends after tapping on the second icon, arrow shaped.

If recipient selects My Story option, then your snap will be selected for my story, which can be later viewed for 24-hours.

# How can you View Snapbacks?

Snapbacks as informed previously are unread snaps. Now learn how can you view them? To view, simply go to Main screen containing menu option, then select square or numbered icon provided at the bottom left corner of the screen. This way, you can see list of feed or thread of all snaps that you have sent along with replies which is called snapbacks plus the new snaps received from friends. You can tap on anything to view for some seconds, because snaps disappear after some time in snapchat.

When you find some extra-ordinary snap and you don't want see it getting lost, simply take screenshot to save it in your system. Recipient will get a notification that you took its screenshot. You can even replay I for free once in a day. Additional replays can be purchased by pressing and holding on the snap you viewed just now. Replay action should be on immediate basis.

Feed OR view screen which you viewed recently will show list of snaps that you sent to your friends. For example, if you have read any snap, an arrow icon will start appearing next to the snap you have read. Not only this, you will get a notification whether recipient took its screenshot or not. In case of replay, icon with replay option will be displayed just next to your name.

## How to Send Stories?

Story is basically continuous part of snap that exists for 24-hours in user's system. This can later be broadcasted to friends and followers or fans. You simply have to tap the icon coating story, provided next to download icon of preview screen. Story allows followers to see your snaps for whole day without putting any restrictions on number of times he or she can see the snaps. You can even keep a track of all who views your storyline.

There is one more way that allows you to send your story. Here, you need to tap send icon after clicking picture. You don't have to select every friend instead, you can simply click My Story option.

Settings allows you to change recipient name in case you don't want to show your story to specific friends.

## How to View Story?

Story once framed can be viewed with the tap of 3-Line icon available on camera screen.

This will take you to screen containing Stories and a Contact List, sometimes unread stories too. Once you see all recent stories, recent column will disappear. However, stories can still be viewed through contact list by scrolling down to the bottom.

In case, you are creating your account on snapchat for official reasons, don't ever put cartoon symbols next to your account name, as this will make your impressions highly unprofessional. For example, some of well-known personalities like Jared Leto an actor by profession has put cactus image next to his name.

Story screen allows you to see Snapchat content along with original programming using Discover section located at the top of screen. You can simply tap on any entertaining publishers, like Comedy Central, in order to launch their channel and see content stream chosen by them to exclusively broadcast through Snapchat.

# How to View Scores?

Scores as already explained defines total amount of snaps sent and received. If you want to view your scope on snapchat, you simply need to swipe camera screen down and this will show your score just next to your account name present below the logo of Snapchat. You can even view total scores of your friends account by tapping screen displaying their names in your contact list.

## How to Chat with friends?

Not only snaps and stories, you can send messages to your friend also.

If you want to access chat feature, simply swipe left side of your camera screen. If you want to send any message to one of your friends, you need to go to contact list, tap your friend's name and then go to chat icon. If you recently sent message to some friend then his or her name will appear in the recent list that appear on chat screen for starting chat again, you simply need to swipe the screen from left side.

You can also tap yellow camera in message pane that is provided at the right side of text box. This can be used to take snaps and later send it to a friend. Image sending is another option that can be used to select images from gallery.

## How to use HERE?

HERE is a sub feature used to do live video chats with already existing friends. You can access this feature by pressing the blue camera button provided on the right side of your message thread. While normal chat, this button is yellow in color and for video, it will automatically turn to blue. You can even broadcast your live audio and video by pressing and holding this blue camera button.

Video chat can be done either when your camera if facing you or when it is away from you. One great thing that this HERE has locking facility. While you are doing video chat, you can use the lock feature to avoid holding thumb while your chat is broadcasted.

Photo credit:http://tecnotitlan. net/wp-content/uploads/2013/11/snapchat. jpg

# Can be used to Send money?

In 2014, Snapchat launched Snapcash in partnership with Square. This app allows you to send money to your friends or you can use debit card to make payments for goods and services purchased.

# How you can pay using debit card?

Go to settings and type your debit card number under settings, then go to contacts containing message of your friend and type dollar sign plus the amount like this $12. 50. Then click the green money button to start transaction.

Photo credit: http://1.bp.blogspot.com/-VOPKCoRjmoA/VDqyGHHYPhI/AAAAAAAAzXE/Hj0UKeB6YMM/s1600/safet-first-snapchat.Jpg

Safety of your debit card is guaranteed. Square, a well-known mobile payments company founded by Jack in 2009 secures your details. So, you can initiate payments without any worry of losing your hard earned money in these transactions. Snapcashapp via Square is openly-available to all people using snapchat option especially in US and paying for goods with a debit card. Minimum age for money transaction is 18 years or older than that.

Photo credits: http://clickwowdesigns.com/wp-content/uploads/2013/07/snapchat.Jpg

# How to Apply for Lenses?

While taking selfies with camera screen, you need to press and hold your face in order to activate a completely new feature, which is called Lenses. This contains facial recognition software that changes your original expression and modifies it by introducing some effects to add beauty to your face. Once you activate lenses, a spider web-thing will come, covering all over your face.

7 different options will come just next to the shutter icon giving 7 options to make changes in your face and picture beautifying your selfies beyond your imaginations. You can

20

select any option and modify your image by following instructions guided by them from time to time. Lenses can be changed by swiping from left side. In case, you are not satisfied with the lens design, you can still purchase it.

## How to get Extra Replays?

Around 2 years back, Snapchat added a new Replay feature as a part of Additional Services found under settings that allows users to review their snaps for one more time.

Generally, users get one replay option in a day, but now people living in US and accessing snapchat can buy extra replays to make it to three replays by paying $0.99. This allows them to replay snaps that they want to see again.

## What is Snapchat Discover and How to use it?

In case, you are looking for any story, then Snapchat Discover is an amazing way of finding it through specific editorial teams. If we want to access this Discover, go to camera screen and swipe from left side and then go to new circle shaped Discover icon at the top-right corner.

You can find editorial team in form of a grid containing Snapchat's snap channels, Cosmo, CNN, Daily Mail, People, etc. You can open any one of these editions by mere tapping. Swiping from left side will allow you to browse through snaps and many other options to entertain yourself with.

Every edition that you see on screen is refreshed on daily basis, to bring something new and interesting each day, to maintain charm of this app.

## Is Snapchat making its series content?

Yes. Snapchat is starting its programming by introducing series of contents for itself.

Literally Can't Even, Snapchats first series, the original one was created by Sasha Spielberg, the daughter of well-known film director and producer Steven Spielberg and Goldwyn, the daughter of film producer John Goldwyn.

These creators have also starred series of "comedic versions of themselves" based in Los Angeles. Literally Can't Even episodes lasted for 5-minutes long and were premiered on 31 January via Snapchat's snap Channel, launched newly. Every Saturday, new episodes were debuted.

Photo credits: http://i.ytimg.com/vi/-NKOsYp1rLc/hqdefault.jpg

# Cool tips and secrets to Snapchat app

Snapchat is becoming immensely popular these days. With more than 2 billion snaps that are sent everyday with self-destructing capability, this app is all-time favorites of millions of successful users who are getting entertained on daily basis. This app is a compact package of entertainment with addictive properties that forces users to use this app on frequent basis. For beginners, snapchat may look like instant photo or video sending app but it has many other cool features that are yet to unveil in this secret guide of using snapchat app.

Hope you are curious enough to know more about these secrets to use this app in an all-together different way.

1. **You can Use 2 filters in one go**

   Filters increases your interest and scope of using this free app Snapchat and gives you a never ending experience of viewing amazing photos and video that destructs automatically in seconds.

   *Do u know you can use two filters at one time?*

Yes, this is true. You can inculcate image filter with the data filter by applying first filter on a snap and holding your one finger on the screen and other one, to choose the second filter.

## 2.  Use  Travel Mode to save data

Snapchat is very interesting and make its users addictive to it. This will kill user's time and battery resulting in battery discharge for other important business work. To avoid this problem, Snapchatapp comes with a "Travel Mode" that reduces battery consumption by decreasing the amount of mobile data, which is otherwise used for accessing snapchat. When you activate Travel Mode, you will have to manually tap the screen to load snaps or stories like content. This mode is disabled by default and so you can enable it in additional services.

## 3.  Introduce hilarious effects to your selfies using cool Lenses

Selfie trend has become most popular these days. People go to any place and click their selfies to update their status on snapchat like apps. You can add hilarious effects to these selfies to gain more attention by using various types of lenses. These kinds of lenses improve your selfies and videos. How to use lenses has been already explained in this book. While taking selfies from front facing camera, you simply need to press and hold camera viewfinder screen and see multiple lenses to enhance your selfies and video quality. You can choose any of funny lens out of many other lenses like "Open your mouth" etc to add hilariousness to your photo or video. Before using these lenses, keep your face in upright position or as per demand of the lens.

4.  **Look for rewind and Slow-mo amazing filters**

    Snapchat not only includes amazing features but also some cool filters like Rewind and Slow-mo. You can simply swipe across various filters after recording your video. You will see 3 icons displaying a snail, a rabbit and last a rewind button.

    Snail filter will take your video shot to slow-mo video. Video playback speed can be increased via Rabbit filter and last but not the least, rewind filter as the name suggest will rewind or reverse your video.

5. **Using Taps to Switch between camera modes**

You can switch from rear camera to front camera using taps. Double tap camera viewfinder to switch between different camera modes with ease.

6. **Replying to Stories**

Snapchat story is a 24 hour game displaying your photos or clicked throughout the day. Replying to these story is a pretty easy task. You can add any photo, by simply pressing + button provide at the time of clicking snaps.

Your friends can view your story and even reply accordingly. Taking an example of viewing your friend's story and you want to express your feelings or put comments against any snap. To do this, you simply need to swipe the bottom screen and type message you want to reply and then press enter. This will allow you to send reply along with the image itself.

## 7. Activate night camera mode

You can now click brighter images even in case of low or dim lights. Yes, you heard it right Users can now use night mode and click clear pictures even at night or at areas, where there is least availability of lighting.

Snapchat app comes with built-in night camera mode that automatically turns on when lighting is poor or dark.

## 8. You can use Gallery to send photos

Snapchat recently updated this feature and offers facility to send images stored in your systems' Gallery. While chatting, you can press yellow button to access camera. You will find one icon for clicking images in viewfinder plus one more that will take your screen to Gallery option in order to select image. These images however, can be sent only when you are in chat room, you cannot send them directly from home screen.

## 9. Initiate video chat live

You can do video chat in Snapchat app. You will see a dark glowing Blue colored button when you are online and the person on other side, with whom you are interested in initiating chat is also online, whereas Yellow button indicates that you can start video chat. To start, you and the other person should press and hold blue button for some time. You will have to hold your fingers until the time you want to make your video chat or else your chat will be disconnected.

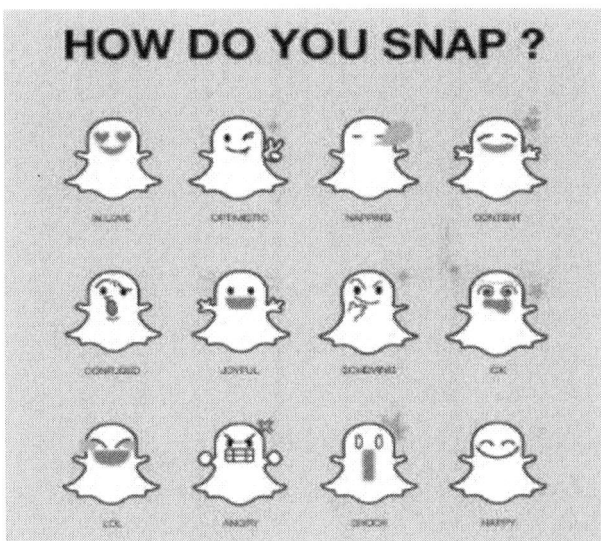

Photo credits: http://acmos.net/wp-content/uploads/2013/07/317086_397218963706400_737118848_n-300x300.png

## 10. New emojis for friends

Snapchat recently introduced "Friend emojis" feature, that was earlier restricted to "Best friends" only. The features will allow you to determine about the person who is your best friend or any common friend who is mutual best friends of your friend and you itself. There are different emojis for best friend, mutual best friend, BFF etc that is mostly seen next to your friend's name. You can go to emojis through Additional Services.

## 11. Importance of Account Log In verification

Snapchat started as a private photo sharing platform but it has recently reported some hacks and scams which have forced developers to increase security and verify details of the users logging in to their account on snapchat. Login verification has thus become an important part of maintaining data and email security of snapchat users. For enabling this login verification feature you need to verify your login details and then tap "Continue" option to move to next step. Verification modules can be either via

SMS or authentication app like Duo or Google Authenticator.

## 12. Use Volume buttons to Control Camera

Volume buttons can be used to click photos while using front facing camera. You simply need to press volume button to capture image and hold it, in case you wish to get videos.

## 13. Story views check

Snapchat has offered view check option for story lovers. This allows user to check total number of views that story have received so far. To check view, swipe <"Stories"> tab provided few distance, away from the home page. Simply Tap "My Story" and swipe bottom of screen in upward direction to get total number of views and even details of people who have viewed it.

## 14. Emojis can be Resized, inverted when used with text messages

Emojis no doubt add fun to your message in humorous way. You can show your happiness, anger and present status using emojis when words are not enough to express your feelings. You can resize, invert emojis according to the availability of space and your mood of sending it. You simply need to add emoji with your message and resize, either increase or decrease it according to the effects it gives on your message. These emojis can be rotated by simply panning your fingers across the screen or emojis itself. Not only emojis, texted data can be resized, inverted text in the same way as emojis does.

Photo credits: https://www. whizsky. com/wp-content/uploads/2015/02/snapchat-musical-snaps-350x200. jpg

## 15. Add music effects to your snapchat videos

Snapchat allows its users to add music to the snaps or videos and create a unique effect on sound and video. You can simply play any song through music player of your system and add it with a text to make a perfect blend of sound and text. While song is being played, you can add videos through snapchat. This will allow you to play your videos with musical effects.

## 16. How to Delete your account?

If unfortunately, your snapchat app gets deleted from your system, no need to worry. Your account will still exist when you download it again. In case you want to delete your account, you need to go to Snapchat website and delete your account manually. Use this link:

https://support.snapchat. com/delete-account

Log In here and fill all credentials, then click "Delete account" option to delete your account forever.

Snapchat Support

# Delete Account

Warning: Account deletion cannot be undone. If you're absolutely sure you want to delete your account, enter your password to continue:

Password

Delete My Account

Photo credits: http://www. bing. com/images/search?q=snapchat+images&view=detailv2&qft=+filterui%3alicense-L2_L3_L4&id=25A0BBC40F7298ED3DB4783BC792A60C55BEA440&selectedIndex=126&ccid=DQULbnvk&simid=608033667689549785&thid=OIP.M0d050b6e7be433b53dac86194d10b720o0&ajaxhist=0

# Understanding ways of using Snapchats' new Features

Daily lenses, Story replies, Slo-mo and rewind filters, Force Touch, New Lenses, Purchase extra replays,Trophies, skipping story or snap, Video Calling, Filters, Replay, Front facing Flash, Special text, Number of friends, are some of the new features that needs attention before starting to use them. We will go one by one to study them in detail:

### How to use Daily lenses

Snapchat by this time, you know that has facility to send videos and snap that self-distrusts after some seconds. Lenses are another important feature that needs consideration after this self-destruction property. Snapchats even received offers from multiple big business tycoons to buy these lenses for real money, but snapchat turned all offers down and rejected the idea of selling its lenses in market. Since then, snapchat has introduced new lenses features by updating them on daily basis instead of giving monotonous lens every day. It keeps removing old lens and replace them by adding new one every time. In case, you make any in-app purchase for lens, then that will stay with you permanently.

**How to learn Story replies**

Snapchat Story is one of the best part of using snapchat app, displaying amazing collection of videos and photos taken over a period of 24 hours, which can be viewed or replayed even by your friends. But how can you replay any specific Snapchat photo or video from story of your friend? Until now, this was a confusing task, but now everything is clear and simpler to make things easier.

Snapchat officially added story replies features in the recent update. This allows you to reply to any particular snap or video when you are viewing your friend story. You simply need to swipe in upward direction from the bottom of the screen. This will open a new chat window. You can type your message here and chat with your friend giving snapshot of the video or photo you're replying against.

This however, is not that bog feature but have made communication easier and least complicated.

**Using Slo-mo and rewind filters**

Latest version of this app allows you to capture your video. After you are done with this, simply swipe in any direction whether left or right until you can see three rewind arrows or a snail symbol for slo-mo. Rewind filter is basically used when you want to add any magical effects like impossible catches when you are throwing ball in a usual manner.

**Using Force Touch**

This feature is quite a basic one and doesn't require any reading through complicated manuals. Force Touch is activated by pressing hard the Snapchat icon and you will simply get options to begin any new chat or add any new friend.

**Using New lenses**

Snapchat keeps adding new lenses. Some of them are available only on "new Android devices".

For lenses, you need to open this app while assuring that you have activated your front facing-camera. If you want to load lenses, press the screen containing your face for longer time. List of lenses will appear and any one can be accessed by scrolling down horizontally. You need to follow some instruction guided time to time.

## Purchasing extra replays

For the time being, only people using snapchat or US Snapchatters have this additional service of purchasing replays. Other people can see replay of only one snap in a day but US Snapchatter can buy 3 snaps viewing capability by spending almost $0.99 for 3 snap a day, which is almost negligible amount. .

## Using Trophies

You can see your personal chat code by Swiping main screen down. This will display a trophy icon, tapping it will show you the trophies that you have unlocked. These trophies are basically your rewards and achievements almost similar to computer games.

There are almost 16 trophies and in case you manage to get only 1, and then try getting more. There is no point in tapping locked trophies as you will have to unlock them first.

## Skipping story or snap

If your device is getting short of memory space, you can skip some of your stories or snaps. If you want to skip any story or snap, then simply hold your one finger on screen, view the snap and move slowly tapping anywhere else on the screen to skip the snap or story you were viewing previously.

## Video calling in SnapChat

Amazingly right, you can do video call through snapchat. If you want to do video chat with your friends simply, swipe the screen just to the right after where you have store your friend's name. In case, you leave the screen, messages from both of you will be deleted to maintain your privacy. The app notifies user of his or her friend's availability and both of them can make a video call by pressing and holding live video chat option.

## Using Filters

Like Instagram, Snapchat app also has filters that can be added to your photos. Filters are not switched ON by default so you need to switch them ON in order to get their benefits

After you have clicked your photo, simply swipe screen from left or right and then a message will pop up asking you to "turn on filters". In case you want to turn on, click "I want filters" button provided at the bottom of the screen. Filter box can then be clicked after going through the "additional services". Now you can use these filters and switch them ON and OFF according to your ease.

## Using Replays

Go to settings of "additional services" by swiping screen from left when on main screen, hitting cog wheel and then selecting manage found under additional services in order to switch ON the replay option. Once you've switched it on. This option can be used after every 24 hours' time.

Others can replay your snaps by default and so this option can't be switched off by users and recipient.

## Using Front facing flash

Flash is mainly used to click picture in dark areas. Rear camera mostly has this features integrated in it.

Additional service menu contains additional Front Facing Flash for clicking selfies or recording video calls using front camera in low light.

This in turn will convert your screen to white in order to provide extra lighting effects to the photo being clicked.

This front facing flash can be switched ON and OFF from the option provided at top left corner of the camera screen.

## Using Special text

In case, you want to add special text caption effects to your snaps, you can do so by using special text option. Additional service menu has this amazing option which Symbol T representing an option symbol to change your text your way.

## Using Number of best friends

You can see your friends list while going through the best friends menu in additional services menu. You simply need to select it and make a choice of number, you want to fix for counting your best friends. The maximum limit in this section has been fixed to 7.

# Removing your Best friends from snapchat list

You can remove your best friend from your friends list of snapchat in a very simple and easy way. But still, you need to learn methodology that will help you remove your friends' contacts without facing any issues.

### Step-1. Review your score

Scores are displayed next to your friends name in your contact list. This represents the number of snaps sent or received by you. To be precise, your score will show the total amount of activities done by you on snapchat since you joined it.

### Step-2. Getting your friends name to Best Friend List

After first step, this step will decide who all your best friends are depending upon the score count.

### Step-3. Your friends score is updated weekly

Snapchat uses specific algorithm to detect the best friend, displaying the scores or number of snaps that have been exchanged between the user and the friends itself. New update features scores in form of 3, 5, 7 which gets updated on weekly basis

You can control your best friends list, by making settings for displaying friend's name you wish to see on your screen. There are many reasons why you want to remove your friends from your friends list.

- You may not be friends now
- Your best friends become available on your public profile that allows everyone to see that he or she is your bet friend, which sometimes may become an odd activity.

So, you can simply protect yourself from these kinds of circumstances by removing these kinds of friends from your best friends list.

## Method to remove People from your friends List

You cannot hide any name from your Best Friends list, but you use some methods that will restrict other friends or followers to see your best friend's name. Simply use block and unblock feature to replace any friend and add new one.

Blocked names can be replaced by the name of other friends of your contact list.

If you want to block someone, follow below mentioned simple instructions:

1. You will see a gear like icon in settings; go for it in order to check your best friends list.

2. This will open a pop up window giving you choices either to block or Delete the person; you want to remove from your contacts.

3. In case, you want to block, click block option.

4. After you successfully block any individual, your score value will reset to 0 automatically.

5. This will remove that person from your friends and contacts lists.

This method is very simple and easy to implement. You can maintain your privacy and block any person without giving him prior notification. So, he or she will not know whether you have blocked him or her or not. Once you block any friend, your score will become 0 showing next to your friends name in your contact list.

This 0 will appear only on your contact list and not on your friends, so he/she have no idea that you blocked him/her.

Now after sometime, if you want to unblock that person, simply scroll down until the lowest part of contacts, where blocked contacts will be highlighted. Now again you will see gear shaped icon next to contacts name, Click it and see unblock option in the next window that pop up.

This way, you can easily block and unblock any friend. If you want to increase your score with any of your friend, do the maximum chats with that person and take your score to a complete new level. Chatting will improve your score and make new friends which can later become your best friends, when score reaches a certain level.

# Top 5 ways to increase Snapchat followers

Make smart decisions and don't fool yourself in the gaming world of snapchat app. Listed below are 5 ways to increase followers and see your score increasing day by day:

1. **Make proper analysis of the app before you invite your friends**

   Hope you have had enough experience working with other social networking apps like Twitter, Facebook, Iinstagram. Before broadcasting any data or image of yours, always review the experience you have had with these previous sites and then move smoothly to create a genuine yet sense making account so as to avoid getting junks. Analyze all features and how to use recently added features so as to master the app before inviting any friend.

2. **You may Invite your friends in order to scan Snapchat screen.**

NIFTY function has completely changes the procedure of getting followers on this site. You can easily use NIFTY on snapchat. You simply have to open snapchat chat. Don't take photo instead click picture of ghost provided at the top of your camera screen. It can be white or yellow in color.

You may be assuming that this feature is important only when both of you and your friend is sitting face to face and carrying their mobiles in hands. But scenario is completely different from what you are thinking right now.

You can click screenshot image of your snapchat screen and invite your friends from other social networking sites like Facebook etc to join you for free. This sounds one of the great ways to transfer your other sites friends to snapchat one.

3. **You may take help from other platforms to show people your funny activities of Snapchat app.**

You can take preview of some of amazing things that you enjoyed doing on snapchat app and ask your follower's to see your activities and reply "How they feel about it?" You can tease your Instagram friends by adding captions on your images through snapchat. Hope this will do wonders in bringing most followers through Instagram and increasing your score count.

Reports even suggest that snapchat has gained much popularity even higher as compared to Vine and Instagram like sites. This app is almost 3 years old and has lagged behind many other apps with some of its unique features.

Taking an example of **Josh Peck** and **Logan Paul**, both are now accessing Snapchat app to get more followers.

4. **Implement your creative skills and use snapchat effectively**

Snapchat like other apps Twitter and Instagram is highly personal and considered best for people with creative and skillful mind. Snapchat inherently story creation gives user option to view his or her photo collection or video collection for 24-hours' time and this is one of the most unique and creative feature that any app have offered so far.

Snapchat app combines random and single events plus series of events that take place in a day in story style. You can either play your images or story to create a new style of your own.

## 5.   Too many friends make result in loss of money.

Many brands hire Snapchat influencers and pay them on daily basis just like big bloggers are paid for featuring any product in their Instagram accounts.

# Using Snapchatfor marketing

Snapchat is one of the most populous apps that have come under the radar of most business hungry people. New marketing strategies have been designed to introduce snapchat as a medium of communicating their services to the end users. Are you still stuck to use snapchat in your business? We would advise some measures that will ease your hurdles of integrating snapchat with your latest marketing strategies.

### 1. Click snaps with a flick of an eye

The very first step that any marketer can think of is using any conventional marketing strategy to promote his brand or product. But this app called snapchat will drive you crazy by its unique features and bound you to use it in the current business.

Snapchat, by this time everyone knows that, is basically used to click images and videos that lasts only for maximum 10 seconds on the screen and self-destructs after that time. This app is a bit different than others available in the market.

Most of top rated companies are taking snapchat as an ultimate option to market their content and maintain its privacy due to its self-destruction nature. These marketers looked for an app that could provide them with in-snap and out-snap feature plus images with a spur of moment display which can be changed with the time to maintain uniqueness of the content.

Taking an example of any game, like NBA basketball game, where players' initial step in the game has no relevance at later stages of the game.

## 2. Giving rewards and discount coupons

Snapchat can be marketed by offering Snappy discounts and attractive coupon messages in order to attain the maximum rating in social media world. Since snapchat messages lasts only for few seconds, you don't have to worry much on the commitment as you can certainly say that offer lasted for that particular period of time.

To maintain trust, you can acknowledge the duration of offer so that customers are not cheated to the initial stages. This will build a relation of trust between you and your customer who can later become your potential follower.

People who have already created their account will have an added advantage of your offer as you will keep them updated on daily basis. You may use some promo codes which can later be redeemed and used to get business proposals.

One of the popular frozen yoghurt brands called 16Handles, launched Snappy NewYear campaign which ran successfully. This campaign motivated users to click their picture while eating yoghurt and get considerable discounts of almost 16%, 50% and in some cases even 100% provided, snap was clicked and showed at the counter in 10 seconds time. This activity became easy only for snapchat users.

### 3. Use snapchat to Preview new range of products

Many users use Facebook, Twitter like apps to showcase their products. This takes time to display all products one by one. Snapchat shows products for 10 seconds and moves to the next snap without consuming much of your time. This app can be utilized to market your products long before it actually enters the real world.

In case you are a clothes designer, you can showcase your designs and asks for customer's feedback. Customer's reviews can be taken positively to make amendments in case required.

Taking an example of well-known Fashion Designer called Rebecca Minkoff used this promotional technique in 2013 to release her Spring 2014 collection. This gave her fans and followers, a new medium to see new collection of products even before products arrival in market.

This technique will bring your followers to your stores even before any other customer visits and see your collection.

## 4. Intimate your followers about your latest offering

If you are running a business, you can smartly use snapchat to inform your customers about your latest offers and deals. You might have come across marketing people in malls where they distribute their cards and invite you for free dinner. These are all marketing tactics to create awareness about their existence and hence the products.

You can inform about your company products and offering in free dinner and hopefully get potential customers for your business. This is however a slow process but brings fruitful results after some time.

Exclusive events can be organized via snapchat inviting Snapchat users to attend the event and look for your offering in that event. You can select some specific customers in order to avoid overspending of money.

## 5. Using background footage or images for promotion.

You can Release footages of pictures or videos that keep running behind-the-scenes and give details to your fans and followers about your offers and product.

Using these images and videos, customers will be more intuitive and attracted towards snapchat offers.

You can also customize messages targeting potential customers and users who love to receive your product details without failure.

Many companies have adopted this marketing strategy to expand their business through snapchat. This allows user to make an easy guess of your products and prepare them for purchasing at the time of release.

# Some Thumb rules that should be followed while using Snapchat

### Rule number-1. Focus on posting cute things.

Every person loves one thing or the other. Post some interesting facts through snapchat to catch attention of fans or followers of that post.

### Rule Number-2. Have complete fun with your friends.

Your friends are your all-time buddies and give you complete refreshment from your hectic work schedule. Don't ever post serious things and try to go crazy and have complete fun on snapchat.

### Rule Number-3. Develop habit of taking screen shots

Screenshot allows you to save pictures or videos sent by your friends. You can view these photos in your past time.

# Some Thumb rules that should not be followed while using Snapchat

**Rule number-1. Don't go for posting long Stories.**

People usually don't have enough time to read or view your long stories. So, keep it short and simple to increase your followers for story if you really want to share your whole day pictures then please move to other social networking sites where you can get a facility of sharing your full day crap activities with friends, relatives and many other unknown people because Snapchat is basically meant for sharing short messages easily and quickly.

**Rule Number-2. Don't post your snaps to all friends all the time**

Keep some snaps secretly and don't ever post all snaps or videos to all friends in your contact list. You can spare some snaps for your special friends whom you consider special from your other friends list.

## Rule Number-3. Never post your selfies in story.

Your selfies for are fun and not sharing with others. You should avoid sharing your selfies as story as this will break your privacy.

# Conclusion

Snapchat however, is a new app and have entered just some time back as compared to other social networking sites, it has really gained popularity and significant fame by its creative features like likes, shares or comments in order to build potential audience, that can likely become your potential followers.

Printed in Great Britain
by Amazon